On the Good of Marriage

On the Good of Marriage

St. Augustine

On the Good of Marriage
© Lighthouse Publishing 2018

Written by: St. Augustine (Nov.13 354 – Aug.28 430)

Translated by: Rev. C. L. Cornish. M.A.

Updated into Modern U.S English by A.M. Overett (b. 1960)

All rights reserved. Without limiting the rights under copyright reserved above, no part of this publication may be reproduced, stored in a retrieval system, or transmitted, in any form or by any means (electronic, mechanical, photocopying, recording or otherwise), without the prior written permission of the copyright owner of this book.

Published by
Lighthouse Christian Publishing
SAN 257-4330
5531 Dufferin Drive
Savage, Minnesota, 55378
United States of America

www.lighthousechristianpublishing.com

Introductory Notice.

This treatise, and the following, were written against somewhat that still remained of the heresy of Jovinian. S. Aug. mentions this error in b. ii. c. 23, de Nuptiis et Conc. "Jovinianus," he says, "who a few years since tried to found a new heresy, said that the Catholics favored the Manichæans, because in opposition to him they preferred holy Virginity to Marriage." And in his book on Heresies, c. 82. "That heresy took its rise from one Jovinianus, a Monk, in our own time, when we were yet young." And he adds that it was soon overborne and extinguished, say about A.D.390, having been condemned first at Rome, then at Milan. There are letters of Pope Siricius on the subject to the Church of Milan, and the answer sent him by the Synod of Milan, at which St. Ambrose presided. Jerome had refuted Jovinian, but was said to have attempted the defense of the excellency of the virgin state, at the expense of condemning marriage. That Augustin might not be subject to any such complaint or calumny, before speaking of the superiority of Virginity, he thought it well to write on the Good of Marriage.

This work we learn to have been finished about the year 401, not only from the order of his Retractations, but also from his books on Genesis after the Letter, begun about that year. For in b. ix. on Genesis, c. 7, where he commends the Good of Marriage, he says: "Now this is threefold, faithfulness, offspring, and the Sacrament. For faithfulness, it is observed, that there be no lying with other man or woman, out of the bond of wedlock: for the offspring, that it be lovingly welcomed, kindly nourished, religiously brought up: for the Sacrament, that marriage be not severed, and that man or woman divorced be not joined to another even for the sake of offspring. This is as it were the rule of Marriages by which rule either fruitfulness is made seemly, or the perverseness of incontinence is brought to order. Upon which since we have sufficiently discoursed in that book, which we lately published, on the Good of Marriage, where we have also distinguished the Widow's continence and the Virgin's excellency, according to the worthiness of their degrees, our pen is not to be now longer occupied." This very work is referred to in Book I. on the Deserts and Remission of Sins, c. 29. — Bened. Ed.

NOTICE.

The Editors are, of course, aware of the danger there is in reading a treatise like the following in a spirit of idle curiosity, and they beg any reader who has not well assured himself that his aim is right and holy to abstain from perusing it. At the same time it must not be forgotten, that something far other than a mere shrinking from subjects offensive to modern delicacy is needed, in order to purify the thoughts with respect to the holy estate of Matrimony. The mind that will but seriously attend to it in that light, will certainly be strengthened against evil suggestions by seeing in the whole subject a field of Christian duty. It seemed further requisite to bring forward a work calculated to remove the imputation so falsely cast on the holy Fathers, that they regarded Matrimony as unholy, and almost agreed with the Manichean view of it, as a defilement and degradation to the Christian. They did, it is true, prefer Virginity to Marriage, but as St. Augustin expressly states, as the "better of two good things," not as though one were good, and the other evil.

In estimating the work and the writer, the age in which it was written must be kept in view, and what that age required must not be imputed as a fault to him or to his religion. And perhaps what was written for another age may serve the more safely towards our improvement and guidance from the very circumstance that the style and manner of antiquity has become a kind of veil, which takes off somewhat from the strength and vividness of first impressions, and leaves the mind more at liberty to use what is laid before it as it will, than a more modern way of speaking would be likely to do. Let that liberty be used rightly and conscientiously, and the effect of reading will be good.—Eds. of the Oxford Library.

1. For as much as each man is a part of the human race, and human nature is something social, and hath for a great and natural good, the power also of friendship; on this account God willed to create all men out of one, in order that they might be held in their society not only by likeness of kind, but also by bond of kindred. Therefore, the first natural bond of human society is man and wife. Nor did God create these each by himself, and join them together as alien by birth: but He created the one out of the other, setting a sign also of the power of the union in the side, whence she was drawn, was formed. For they are joined one to another side by side, who walk together, and look together whither they walk. Then follows the conection of fellowship in children, which is the one alone worthy fruit, not of the union of male and female, but of the sexual intercourse. For it were possible that there should exist in either sex, even without such intercourse, a certain friendly and true union of the one ruling, and the other obeying.

2. Nor is it now necessary that we enquire, and put forth a definite opinion on that question, whence could exist the progeny of the first men, whom God had blessed, saying, "Increase, and be ye multiplied, and fill the earth;" if they had not sinned, whereas their bodies by sinning deserved the condition of death, and there can be no sexual intercourse save of mortal bodies. For there have existed several and different opinions on this matter; and if we must examine, which of them be rather agreeable to the truth of Divine Scriptures, there is matter for a lengthened discussion. Whether, therefore, without intercourse, in some other way, had they not sinned, they would have had sons, from the gift of the Almighty

Creator, Who was able to create themselves also without parents, Who was able to form the Flesh of Christ in a virgin womb, and (to speak even to unbelievers themselves) Who was able to bestow on bees a progeny without sexual intercourse; or whether many things there were spoken by way of mystery and figure, and we are to understand in another sense what is written, "Fill the earth, and rule over it;" that is, that it should come to pass by fullness and perfection of life and power, so that the very increase and multiplication, whereby it is said, "Increase, and be ye multiplied," be understood to be by advance of mind, and abundance of virtue, as it is set in the Psalm, "Thou shall multiply me in my soul by virtue;" and that succession of progeny was not given unto man, save after that, by reason of sin, there was to be hereafter departure in death: or whether the body was not made spiritual in the case of these men, but at the first animal, in order that by merit of obedience it might after become spiritual, to lay hold of immortality, not after death, which by the malice of the devil entered into the world, and was made the punishment of sin; but after that change, which the Apostle signifies, when he says, "Then we living, who remain, together with them, shall be caught up in the clouds, to meet Christ, into the air," that we may understand both that those bodies of the first pair were mortal, in the first forming, and yet that they would not have died, had they not sinned, as God had threatened: even as if He should threaten a wound, in that the body was capable of wounds; which yet would not have happened, unless what He had forbidden were done. Thus, therefore, even through sexual intercourse there might take place generations of such bodies, as up to a certain point should have increase, and yet should not pass into old age; or even into old age, and yet not into death; until the earth were filled with that multiplication of the blessing. For if to the garments of the Israelites God granted their proper state without any wearing away during forty years, how much more would He grant unto the bodies of such as obeyed His command a certain most happy temperament of sure state, until they should be changed for the better, not by death of the man, whereby the body is abandoned by the soul, but by a blessed change from mortality to immortality, from an animal to a spiritual quality. Of these opinions which be true, or whether some other or others yet may be formed out of these words, were a long matter to enquire and discuss.

3. This we now say, that, according to this condition of being born and dying, which we know, and in which we have been created, the marriage of male and female is some good; the compact whereof divine Scripture so commends, as that neither is it allowed one put away by her husband to marry, so long as her husband lives: nor is it allowed one put away by his wife to marry another, unless she who have separated from him be dead. Therefore, concerning the good of marriage, which the Lord also confirmed in the Gospel, not only in that He forbade to put away a wife, save because of fornication, but also in that He came by invitation to a marriage, there is good ground to inquire for what reason it be a good. And this seems not to me to be merely on account of the begetting of children, but also on account of the natural society itself in a difference of sex. Otherwise it would not any longer be called marriage in the case of old persons, especially if either they had lost sons, or had given birth to none. But now in good, although aged,

marriage, albeit there hath withered away the glow of full age between male and female, yet there lives in full vigor the order of charity between husband and wife: because, the better they are, the earlier they have begun by mutual consent to contain from sexual intercourse with each other: not that it should be matter of necessity afterwards not to have power to do what they would, but that it should be matter of praise to have been unwilling at the first, to do what they had power to do. If therefore there be kept good faith of honor, and of services mutually due from either sex, although the members of either be languishing and almost corpse-like, yet of souls duly joined together, the chastity continues, the purer by how much it is the more proved, the safer, by how much it is the calmer. Marriages have this good also, that carnal or youthful incontinence, although it be faulty, is brought unto an honest use in the begetting of children, in order that out of the evil of lust the marriage union may bring to pass some good. Next, in that the lust of the flesh is repressed, and rages in a way more modestly, being tempered by parental affection. For there is interposed a certain gravity of glowing pleasure, when in that wherein husband and wife cleave to one another, they have in mind that they be father and mother.

4. There is this further, that in that very debt which married persons pay one to another, even if they demand it with somewhat too great intemperance and incontinence, yet they owe faith alike one to another. Unto which faith the Apostle allows so great right, as to call it "power," saying, "The woman hath not power of her own body, but the man; again in like manner also the man hath not power of his own body, but the woman."

But the violation of this faith is called adultery, when either by instigation of one's own lust, or by consent of lust of another, there is sexual intercourse on either side with another against the marriage compact: and thus faith is broken, which, even in things that are of the body, and mean, is a great good of the soul: and therefore it is certain that it ought to be preferred even to the health of the body, wherein even this life of ours is contained. For, although a little chaff in comparison of much gold is almost nothing; yet faith, when it is kept pure in a matter of chaff, as in gold, is not therefore less because it is kept in a lesser matter. But when faith is employed to commit sin, it were strange that we should have to call it faith; however of what kind so ever it be, if also the deed be done against it, it is the worse done; save when it is on this account abandoned, that there may be a return unto true and lawful faith, that is, that sin may be amended, by correction of perverseness of the will. As if any, being unable alone to rob a man, should find a partner in his iniquity, and make an agreement with him to do it together, and to divide the spoil; and, after the crime hath been committed, should take off the whole to himself alone. That other grieves and complains that faith hath not been kept with him, but in his very complaint he ought to consider, that he himself rather ought to have kept faith with human society in a good life, and not to make unjust spoil of a man, if he feels with how great injustice it hath failed to be kept with himself in a fellowship of sin. Forsooth the former, being faithless in both instances, must assuredly be judged the more wicked. But, if he had been displeased at what they had done ill, and had been on this account unwilling to divide the spoil with his partner in crime, in order that it might be restored to the man, from whom it had been taken, not even a faithless man would call him faithless. Thus a woman, if, having broken her marriage faith, she keep faith with her adulterer, is certainly evil: but, if not even with her adulterer, worse. Further, if she repent her of her sin, and returning to marriage chastity, renounce all adulterous compacts and resolutions, I count it strange if even the adulterer himself will think her one who breaks faith.

5. Also the question is wanting to be asked, when a male and female, neither the one the husband, nor the other the wife, of any other, come together, not for the begetting of children, but, by reason of incontinence, for the mere sexual intercourse, there being between them this faith, that neither he do it with any other woman, nor she with any other man, whether it is to be called marriage. And perhaps this may, not without reason, be called marriage, if it shall be the resolution of both parties until the death of one, and if the begetting of children, although they came not together for that cause, yet they shun not, so as either to be unwilling to have children born to them, or even by some evil work to use means that they be not born. But, if either both, or one, of these be wanting, I find not how we can call it marriage. For, if a man should take unto him any one for a time, until he find another worthy either of his honors or of his means, to marry as his compeer; in his soul itself he is an adulterer, and that not with her whom he is desirous of finding, but with her, with whom he so lies, as not to have with her the partnership of a husband. Whence she also herself, knowing and willing this, certainly acts unchastely in having intercourse with him, with whom she has not the compact of a wife. However, if she keep to

him faith of bed, and after he shall have married, have no thought of marriage herself, and prepare to contain herself altogether from any such work, perhaps I should not dare lightly to call her an adulteress; but who shall say that she sins not, when he is aware that she has intercourse with a man, not being his wife? But further, if from that intercourse, so far as pertains to herself, she has no wish but for sons, and suffers unwilling whatever she suffers beyond the cause of begetting; there are many matrons to whom she is to be preferred; who, although they are not adulteresses, yet force their husbands, for the most part also wishing to exercise continence, to pay the due of the flesh, not through desire of children, but through glow of lust making an intemperate use of their very right; in whose marriages, however, this very thing, that they are married, is a good. For this purpose are they married, that the lust being brought under a lawful bond, should not float at large without form and loose; having of itself weakness of flesh that cannot be curbed, but of marriage fellowship of faith that cannot be dissolved; of itself encroachment of immoderate intercourse, of marriage a way of chastely begetting. For, although it be shameful to wish to use a husband for purposes of lust, yet it is honorable to be unwilling to have intercourse save with a husband, and not to give birth to children save from a husband. There are also men incontinent to that degree, that they spare not their wives even when pregnant. Therefore whatever that is immodest, shameless, base, married persons do one with another, is the sin of the persons, not the fault of marriage.

6. Further, in the very case of the more immoderate requirement of the due of the flesh, which the

Apostle enjoins not on them by way of command, but allows to them by way of leave, that they have intercourse also beside the cause of begetting children; although evil habits impel them to such intercourse, yet marriage guards them from adultery or fornication. For neither is that committed because of marriage, but is pardoned because of marriage. Therefore, married persons owe one another not only the faith of their sexual intercourse itself, for the begetting of children, which is the first fellowship of the human kind in this mortal state; but also, in a way, a mutual service of sustaining one another's weakness, in order to shun unlawful intercourse: so that, although perpetual continence be pleasing to one of them, he may not, save with consent of the other. For thus far also, "The wife hath not power of her own body, but the man: in like manner also the man hath not power of his own body, but the woman." That that also, which, not for the begetting of children, but for weakness and incontinence, either he seeks of marriage, or she of her husband, they deny not the one or the other; lest by this they fall into damnable seductions, through temptation of Satan, by reason of incontinence either of both, or of whichever of them. For intercourse of marriage for the sake of begetting hath not fault; but for the satisfying of lust, but yet with husband or wife, by reason of the faith of the bed, it hath venial fault: but adultery or fornication hath deadly fault, and, through this, continence from all intercourse is indeed better even than the intercourse of marriage itself, which takes place for the sake of begetting. But because that Continence is of larger desert, but to pay the due of marriage is no crime, but to demand it beyond the necessity of begetting is a venial fault, but to commit fornication or adultery is a crime to be punished; charity of the married ought to beware, lest whilst it seek for itself occasion of larger honor, it do that for its partner which cause condemnation. "For whosoever putted away his wife, except for the cause of fornication, makes her to commit adultery." To such a degree is that marriage compact entered upon a matter of a certain sacrament, that it is not made void even by separation itself, since, so long as her husband lives, even by whom she hath been left, she commits adultery, in case she be married to another: and he who hath left her, is the cause of this evil.

7. But I marvel, if, as it is allowed to put away a wife who is an adulteress, so it be allowed, having put her away, to marry another. For holy Scripture causes a hard knot in this matter, in that the Apostle says, that, by commandment of the Lord, the wife ought not to depart from her husband, but, in case she shall have departed, to remain unmarried, or to be reconciled to her husband; whereas surely she ought not to depart and remain unmarried, save from a husband that is an adulterer, lest by withdrawing from him, who is not an adulterer, she cause him to commit adultery. But perhaps she may justly be reconciled to her husband, either he being to be borne with, if she cannot contain herself, or being now corrected. But I see not how the man can have permission to marry another, in case he have left an adulteress, when a woman has not to be married to another, in case she have left an adulterer. And, this being the case, so strong is that bond of fellowship in married persons, that, although it be tied for the sake of begetting children, not even for the sake of begetting children is it loosed. For it is in a man's power to put away a wife that is barren, and marry one of whom to have children. And yet it is not

allowed; and now indeed in our times, and after the usage of Rome, neither to marry in addition, so as to have more than one wife living: and, surely, in case of an adulteress or adulterer being left, it would be possible that more men should be born, if either the woman were married to another, or the man should marry another. And yet, if this be not lawful, as the Divine Rule seems to prescribe, who is there but it must make him attentive to learn, what is the meaning of this so great strength of the marriage bond? Which I by no means think could have been of so great avail, were it not that there were taken a certain sacrament of some greater matter from out this weak mortal state of men, so that, men deserting it, and seeking to dissolve it, it should remain unshaken for their punishment. Seeing that the compact of marriage is not done away by divorce intervening; so that they continue wedded persons one to another, even after separation; and commit adultery with those, with whom they shall be joined, even after their own divorce, either the woman with a man, or the man with a woman. And yet, save in the City of our God, in His Holy Mount, the case is not such with the wife. But, that the laws of the Gentiles are otherwise, who is there that knows not; where, by the interposition of divorce, without any offense of which man takes cognizance, both the woman is married to whom she will, and the man marries whom he will. And something like this custom, on account of the hardness of the Israelites, Moses seems to have allowed, concerning a bill of divorcement. In which matter there appears rather a rebuke, than an approval, of divorce.

8. "Honorable," therefore, "is marriage in all, and the bed undefiled." And this we do not so call a good, as

that it is a good in comparison of fornication: otherwise there will be two evils, of which the second is worse: or fornication will also be a good, because adultery is worse: for it is worse to violate the marriage of another, than to cleave unto an harlot: and adultery will be a good, because incest is worse; for it is worse to lie with a mother than with the wife of another: and, until we arrive at those things, which, as the Apostle saith, "it is a shame even to speak of," all will be good in comparison of what are worse. But who can doubt that this is false? Therefore marriage and fornication are not two evils, whereof the second is worse: but marriage and continence are two goods, whereof the second is better, even as this temporal health and sickness are not two evils, whereof the second is worse; but that health and immortality are two goods, whereof the second is better. Also knowledge and vanity are not two evils, whereof vanity is the worse: but knowledge and charity are two goods, whereof charity is the better. For "knowledge shall be destroyed," saith the Apostle: and yet it is necessary for this time: but "charity shall never fail." Thus also this mortal begetting, on account of which marriage takes place, shall be destroyed: but freedom from all sexual intercourse is both angelic exercise here, and continues forever. But as the repasts of the Just are better than the fasts of the sacrilegious, so the marriage of the faithful is to be set before the virginity of the impious. However neither in that case is repast preferred to fasting, but righteousness to sacrilege; nor in this, marriage to virginity, but faith to impiety. For this end the righteous, when need is, take their repast, that, as good masters, they may give to their slaves, i.e., their bodies, what is just and fair: but for this end the sacrilegious fast, that they may serve devils. Thus for this end the faithful are married, that they may be chastely joined unto husbands, but for this end the impious are virgins, that they may commit fornication away from the true God. As, therefore, that was good, which Martha was doing, being engaged in the ministering unto the Saints, but that better, which Mary, her sister, sitting at the feet of the Lord, and hearing His word; thus we praise the good of Susanna in married chastity, but yet we set before her the good of the widow Anna, and, much more, of the Virgin Mary. It was good that they were doing, who of their substance were ministering necessaries unto Christ and His disciples: but better, who left all their substance, that they might be freer to follow the same Lord. But in both these cases of good, whether what these, or whether what Martha and Mary were doing, the better could not be done, unless the other had been passed over or left. Whence we are to understand, that we are not, on this account, to think marriage an evil, because, unless there be abstinence from it, widowed chastity, or virgin purity, cannot be had. For neither on this account was what Martha was doing evil, because, unless her sister abstained from it, she could not do what was better: nor on this account is it evil to receive a just man or a prophet into one's house, because he, who wills to follow Christ unto perfection, ought not even to have a house, in order to do what is better.

9. Truly we must consider, that God gives us some goods, which are to be sought for their own sake, such as wisdom, health, friendship: but others, which are necessary for the sake of somewhat, such as learning, meat, drink, sleep, marriage, sexual intercourse. For of these certain are necessary for the sake of wisdom, as

learning: certain for the sake of health, as meat and drink and sleep: certain for the sake of friendship, as marriage or sexual intercourse: for hence subsists the propagation of the human kind, wherein friendly fellowship is a great good. These goods, therefore, which are necessary for the sake of something else, whoso uses not for this purpose, wherefore they were instituted, sins; in some cases venially, in other cases damnably. But whoso uses them for this purpose, wherefore they were given doeth well. Therefore, to whomsoever they are not necessary, if he use them not, he doeth better. Wherefore, these goods, when we have need, we do well to wish; but we do better not to wish than to wish: because ourselves are in a better state, when we account them not necessary. And on this account it is good to marry, because it is good to beget children, to be a mother of a family: but it is better not to marry, because it is better not to stand in need of this work, in order to human fellowship itself. For such is the state of the human race now, that (others, who contain not, not only being taken up with marriage, but many also waxing wanton through unlawful concubinages, the Good Creator working what is good out of their evils) there fails not numerous progeny, and abundant succession, out of which to procure holy friendships. Whence we gather, that, in the first times of the human race, chiefly for the propagation of the People of God, through whom the Prince and Savior of all people should both be prophesied of, and be born, it was the duty of the Saints to use this good of marriage, not as to be sought for its own sake, but necessary for the sake of something else: but now, whereas, in order to enter upon holy and pure fellowship, there is on all sides from out all nations an overflowing fullness of spiritual kindred, even they who wish to contract marriage only for the sake of children, are to be admonished, that they use rather the larger good of continence.

10. But I am aware of some that murmur: What, say they, if all men should abstain from all sexual intercourse, whence will the human race exist? Would that all would this, only in "charity out of a pure heart, and good conscience, and faith unfeigned;" much more speedily would the City of God be filled, and the end of the world hastened. For what else doth the Apostle, as is manifest, exhort to, when he saith, speaking on this head, "I would that all were as myself;" or in that passage, "But this I say, brethren, the time is short: it remains that both they who have wives, be as though not having: and they who weep, as though not weeping: and they who rejoice, as though not rejoicing: and they who buy, as though not buying: and they who use this world as though they use it not. For the form of this world passes by. I would have you without care." Then he adds, "Whoso is without a wife thinks of the things of the Lord, how to please the Lord: but whoso is joined in marriage, thinks of the things of the world, how to please his wife: and a woman that is unmarried and a virgin is different: she that is unmarried is anxious about the things of the Lord, to be holy both in body and spirit: but she that is married, is anxious about the things of the world, how to please her husband." Whence it seems to me, that at this time, those only, who contain not, ought to marry, according to that sentence of the same Apostle, "But if they contain not, let them be married: for it is better to be married than to burn."

11. And yet not to these themselves is marriage a sin; which, if it were chosen in comparison of fornication, would be a less sin than fornication, and yet would be a sin. But now what shall we say against the plainest speech of the Apostle, saying, "Let her do what she will; she sinned not, if she be married;" and, "If thou shalt have taken a wife, thou hast not sinned: and, if a virgin shall have been married, she sinned not." Hence surely it is not lawful now to doubt that marriage is no sin. Therefore, the Apostle allowed not marriage as matter "of pardon:" for who can doubt that it is extremely absurd to say, that they have not sinned, unto whom "pardon" is granted. But he allows, as matter of "pardon," that sexual intercourse, which takes place through incontinence, not alone for the begetting of children, and, at times, not at all for the begetting of children; and it is not that marriage forces this to take place, but that it procures pardon for it; provided however it be not so in excess as to hinder what ought to be set aside as seasons of prayer, nor be changed into that use which is against nature, on which the Apostle could not be silent, when speaking of the excessive corruptions of unclean and impious men. For necessary sexual intercourse for begetting is free from blame, and itself is alone worthy of marriage. But that which goes beyond this necessity, no longer follows reason, but lust. And yet it pertains to the character of marriage, not to exact this, but to yield it to the partner, lest by fornication the other sin damnably. But, if both are set under such lust, they do what is plainly not matter of marriage. However, if in their intercourse they love what is honest more than what is dishonest, that is, what is matter of marriage more than what is not matter of marriage, this is allowed to them on the authority of the Apostle as matter

of pardon: and for this fault, they have in their marriage, not what sets them on to commit it, but what entreats pardon for it, if they turn not away from them the mercy of God, either by not abstaining on certain days, that they may be free to pray, and through this abstinence, as through fasting, may commend their prayers; or by changing the natural use into that which is against nature, which is more damnable when it is done in the case of husband or wife.

12. For, whereas that natural use, when it passes beyond the compact of marriage, that is, beyond the necessity of begetting, is pardonable in the case of a wife, damnable in the case of a harlot; that which is against nature is execrable when done in the case of a harlot, but more execrable in the case of a wife. Of so great power is the ordinance of the Creator, and the order of Creation, that, in matters allowed us to use, even when the due measure is exceeded, it is far more tolerable, than, in what are not allowed, either a single, or rare excess. And, therefore, in a matter allowed, want of moderation, in a husband or wife, is to be borne with, in order that lust break not forth into a matter that is not allowed. Hence is it also that he sins far less, who is ever so unceasing in approaches to his wife, than he who approaches ever so seldom to commit fornication. But, when the man shall wish to use the member of the wife not allowed for this purpose, the wife is more shameful, if she suffer it to take place in her own case, than if in the case of another woman. Therefore, the ornament of marriage is chastity of begetting, and faith of yielding the due of the flesh: this is the work of marriage, this the Apostle defends from every charge, in saying, "Both if thou shall have taken a wife,

thou hast not sinned: and if a virgin shall have been married, she sinned not:" and, "Let her do what she will: she sinned not if she be married." But an advance beyond moderation in demanding the due of either sex, for the reasons which I have stated above, is allowed to married persons as matter of pardon.

13. What therefore he says, "She, that is unmarried, thinketh of the things of the Lord, that she may be holy both in body and spirit;" we are not to take in such sense, as to think that a chaste Christian wife is not holy in body. Forsooth unto all the faithful it was said, "Know ye not that your bodies are a temple of the Holy Ghost within you, Whom ye have from God?" Therefore, the bodies also of the married are holy, so long as they keep faith to one another and to God. And that this sanctity of either of them, even an unbelieving partner does not stand in the way of, but rather that the sanctity of the wife profits the unbelieving husband, and the sanctity of the husband profits the unbelieving wife, the same Apostle is witness, saying, "For the unbelieving husband is sanctified in the wife, and the unbelieving wife is sanctified in a brother." Wherefore that was said according to the greater sanctity of the unmarried than of the married, unto which there is also due a greater reward, according as, the one being a good, the other is a greater good: inasmuch as also she has this thought only, how to please the Lord. For it is not that a female who believes, keeping married chastity, thinks not how to please the Lord; but assuredly less so, in that she thinks of the things of the world, how to please her husband. For this is what he would say of them, that they may, in a certain way, find themselves obliged by marriage to think of the things

of the world, how to please their husbands.

14. And not without just cause a doubt is raised, whether he said this of all married women, or of such as so many are, as that nearly all may be thought so to be. For neither doth that, which he saith of unmarried women, "She, that is unmarried, thinks of the things of the Lord, to be holy both in body and spirit:" pertain unto all unmarried women: whereas there are certain widows who are dead, who live in delights. However, so far as regards a certain distinction and, as it were, character of their own, of the unmarried and married; as she deserves the excess of hatred, who containing from marriage, that is, from a thing allowed, does not contain from offenses, either of luxury, or pride, or curiosity and prating; so the married woman is seldom met with, who, in the very obedience of married life, hath no thought save how to please God, by adorning herself, not with plaited hair, or gold and pearls and costly attire, but as becometh women making profession of piety, through a good conversation. Such marriages, forsooth, the Apostle Peter also describes by giving commandment. "In like manner," saith he, "wives obeying their own husbands; in order that, even if any obey not the word, they may be gained without discourse through the conversation of the wives, seeing your fear and chaste conversation: that they be not they that are adorned without with crispings of hair, or clothed with gold or with fair raiment; but that hidden man of your heart, in that unbroken continuance of a quiet and modest spirit, which before the Lord also is rich. For thus certain holy women, who hoped in the Lord, used to adorn themselves, obeying their own husbands: as Sarah obeyed Abraham, calling him Lord: whose daughters ye

are become, when ye do well, and fear not with any vain fear. Husbands in like manner living at peace and in chastity with your wives, both give ye honor as to the weaker and subject vessel, as with co-heirs of grace, and see that your prayers be not hindered." Is it indeed that such marriages have no thought of the things of the Lord, how to please the Lord? But they are very rare: who denies this? And, being, as they are, rare, nearly all the persons who are such, were not joined together in order to be such, but being already joined together became such.

15. For what Christian men of our time being free from the marriage bond, having power to contain from all sexual intercourse, seeing it to be now "a time," as it is written, "not of embracing, but of abstaining from embrace," would not choose rather to keep virginal or widowed continence, than (now that there is no obligation from duty to human society) to endure tribulation of the flesh, without which marriages cannot be (to pass over in silence other things from which the Apostle spares.) But when through desire reigning they shall have been joined together, if they shall after overcome it, because it is not lawful to loose, in such wise as it was lawful not to tie, the marriage bond, they become such as the form of marriage makes profession of, so as that either by mutual consent they ascend unto a higher degree of holiness, or, if both are not such, the one who is such will not be one to exact but to yield the due, observing in all things a chaste and religious concord. But in those times, wherein as yet the mystery of our salvation was veiled in prophetic sacraments, even they who were such before marriage, yet contracted marriage through the duty of begetting children, not overcome by lust, but led by piety, unto

whom if there were given such choice as in the revelation of the New Testament there hath been given, the Lord saying "Whoso can receive, let him receive;" no one doubts that they would have been ready to receive it even with joy, who reads with careful attention what use they made of their wives, at a time when also it was allowed one man to have several, whom he had with more chastity, than any now has his one wife, of these, unto whom we see what the Apostle allows by way of leave. For they had them in the work of begetting children, not "in the disease of desire, as the nations which know not God." And this is so great a thing, that many at this day more easily abstain from all sexual intercourse their whole life through, than, if they are joined in marriage, observe the measure of not coming together except for the sake of children. Forsooth we have many brethren and partners in the heavenly inheritance of both sexes that are continent, whether they be such as have made trial of marriage, or such as are entirely free from all such intercourse: forsooth they are without number: yet, in our familiar discourses with them, whom have we heard, whether of those who are, or of those who have been, married, declaring to us that he has never had sexual intercourse with his wife, save with the hope of conception? What, therefore, the Apostles command the married, this is proper to marriage, but what they allow by way of pardon, or what hinders prayers, this marriage compels not, but bears with.

16. Therefore if haply, (which whether it can take place, I know not; and rather think it cannot take place; but yet, if haply), having taken unto himself a concubine for a time, a man shall have sought sons only from this

same intercourse; neither thus is that union to be preferred to the marriage even of those women, who do this, that is matter of pardon. For we must consider what belongs to marriage, not what belongs to such women as marry and use marriage with less moderation than they ought. For neither if each one so use lands entered upon unjustly and wrongly, as out of their fruits to give large alms, doth he therefore justify rapine: nor if another brood over, through avarice, an estate to which he has succeeded, or which he hath justly gained, are we on this account to blame the rule of civil law, whereby he is made a lawful owner. Nor will the wrongfulness of a tyrannical rebellion deserve praise, if the tyrant treat his subjects with royal clemency: nor will the order of royal power deserve blame, if a king rage with tyrannical cruelty. For it is one thing to wish to use well unjust power, and it is another thing to use unjustly just power. Thus neither do concubines taken for a time, if they be such in order to sons, make their concubinage lawful; nor do married women, if they live wantonly with their husbands, attach any charge to the order of marriage.

17. That marriage can take place of persons first ill joined, an honest decree following after, is manifest. But a marriage once for all entered upon in the City of our God, where, even from the first union of the two, the man and the woman, marriage bears a certain sacramental character, can no way be dissolved but by the death of one of them. For the bond of marriage remains, although a family, for the sake of which it was entered upon, do not follow through manifest barrenness; so that, when now married persons know that they shall not have children, yet it is not lawful for them to separate even for the very

sake of children, and to join themselves unto others. And if they shall so do, they commit adultery with those unto whom they join themselves, but themselves remain husbands and wives. Clearly with the good will of the wife to take another woman, that from her may be born sons common to both, by the sexual intercourse and seed of the one, but by the right and power of the other, was lawful among the ancient fathers: whether it be lawful now also, I would not hastily pronounce. For there is not now necessity of begetting children, as there then was, when, even when wives bare children, it was allowed, in order to a more numerous posterity, to marry other wives in addition, which now is certainly not lawful. For the difference that separates times causes the due season to have so great force unto the justice and doing or not doing anything, that now a man does better, if he marry not even one wife, unless he be unable to contain. But then they married even several without any blame, even those who could much more easily contain, were it not that piety at that time had another demand upon them. For, as the wise and just man, who now desires to be dissolved and to be with Christ, and takes more pleasure in this, the best, now not from desire of living here, but from duty of being useful, takes food that he may remain in the flesh, which is necessary for the sake of others; so to have intercourse with females in right of marriage, was to holy men at that time a matter of duty not of lust.

18. For what food is unto the conservation of the man, this sexual intercourse is unto the conservation of the race: and both are not without carnal delight: which yet being modified, and by restraint of temperance reduced unto the use after nature, cannot be lust. But what

unlawful food is in the supporting of life, this sexual intercourse of fornication or adultery is in the seeking of a family. And what unlawful food is in luxury of belly and throat, this unlawful intercourse is in lust that seeks not a family. And what the excessive appetite of some is in lawful food, this that intercourse that is matter of pardon is in husband and wife. As therefore it is better to die of hunger than to eat things offered unto idols: so it is better to die without children, than to seek a family from unlawful intercourse. But from whatever source men be born, if they follow not the vices of their parents, and worship God aright, they shall be honest and safe. For the seed of man, from out what kind of man so ever, is the creation of God, and it shall fare ill with those who use it ill, yet shall not, itself at any time be evil. But as the good sons of adulterers are no defense of adulteries, so the evil sons of married persons are no charge against marriage. Wherefore as the Fathers of the time of the New Testament taking food from the duty of conservation, although they took it with natural delight of the flesh, were yet in no way compared with the delight of those who fed on what had been offered in sacrifice, or of those who, although the food was lawful, yet took it to excess: so the Fathers of the time of the Old Testament from the duty of conservation used sexual intercourse; and yet that their natural delight, by no means relaxed unto unreasonable and unlawful lust, is not to be compared either with the vileness of fornications, or with the intemperance of married persons. Forsooth through the same vein of charity, now after the spirit, then after the flesh, it was a duty to beget sons for the sake of that mother Jerusalem: but it was naught save the difference of times which made the works of the fathers different. But thus it was necessary that even Prophets, not living after the flesh, should come together after the flesh; even as it was necessary that Apostles also, not living after the flesh, should eat food after the flesh.

19. Therefore as many women as there are now, unto whom it is said, "if they contain not, let them be married," are not to be compared to the holy women then, even when they married. Marriage itself indeed in all nations is for the same cause of begetting sons, and of what character so ever these may be afterward, yet was marriage for this purpose instituted, that they may be born in due and honest order. But men, who contain not, as it were ascend unto marriage by a step of honesty: but they, who without doubt would contain, if the purpose of that time had allowed this, in a certain measure descended unto marriage by a step of piety. And, on this account, although the marriages of both, so far as they are marriages, in that they are for the sake of begetting, are equally good, yet these men when married are not to be compared with those men as married. For these have, what is allowed them by the way of leave, on account of the honesty of marriage, although it pertain not to marriage; that is, the advance which goes beyond the necessity of begetting, which they had not. But neither can these, if haply there be now any found, who neither seek, nor desire, in marriage anything, save that wherefore marriage was instituted, be made equal to those men. For in these the very desire of sons is carnal, but in those it was spiritual, in that it was suited to the sacrament of that time. Forsooth now no one who is made perfect in piety seeks to have sons, save after a spiritual sense; but then it was the work of piety itself to beget sons even after

a carnal sense: in that the begetting of that people was fraught with tidings of things to come, and pertained unto the prophetic dispensation.

20. And on this account, not, so as it was allowed one man to have even several wives, was it allowed one female to have several husbands, not even for the sake of a family, in case it should happen that the woman could bear, the man could not beget. For by a secret law of nature things that stand chief love to be singular; but what are subject are set under, not only one under one, but, if the system of nature or society allow, even several under one, not without becoming beauty. For neither hath one slave so several masters, in the way that several slaves have one master. Thus, we read not that any of the holy women served two or more living husbands: but we read that many females served one husband, when the social state of that nation allowed it, and the purpose of the time persuaded to it: for neither is it contrary to the nature of marriage. For several females can conceive from one man: but one female cannot from several, (such is the power of things principal:) as many souls are rightly made subject unto one God. And on this account there is no True God of souls, save One: but one soul by means of many false gods may commit fornication, but not be made fruitful.

21. But since out of many souls there shall be hereafter one City of such as have one soul and one heart towards God; which perfection of our unity shall be hereafter, after this sojourn in a strange land, wherein the thoughts of all shall neither be hidden one from another, nor shall be in any matter opposed one to another; on this

account the Sacrament of marriage of our time hath been so reduced to one man and one wife, as that it is not lawful to ordain any as a steward of the Church, save the husband of one wife. And this they have understood more acutely who have been of opinion, that neither is he to be ordained, who as a catechumen or as a heathen had a second wife. For it is a matter of sacrament, not of sin. For in baptism all sins are put away. But he who said, "If thou shall have taken a wife, thou hast not sinned; and if a virgin shall have been married, she sinned not:" and, "Let her do what she will, she sinned not, if she be married," hath made it plain enough that marriage is no sin. But on account of the sanctity of the Sacrament, as a female, although it be as a catechumen that she hath suffered violence, cannot after Baptism be consecrated among the virgins of God: so there was no absurdity in supposing of him who had exceeded the number of one wife, not that he had committed any sin, but that he had lost a certain prescript rule of a sacrament necessary not unto desert of good life, but unto the seal of ecclesiastic ordination; and thus, as the many wives of the old Fathers signified our future Churches out of all nations made subject unto one husband, Christ: so our chief-priest, the husband of one wife, signifies unity out of all nations, made subject unto one husband, Christ: which shall then be perfected, when He shall have unveiled the hidden things of darkness, and shall have made manifest the thoughts of the heart, that then each may have praise from God. But now there are manifest, there are hidden, dissensions, even where charity is safe between those, who shall be hereafter one, and in one; which shall then certainly have no existence. As therefore the Sacrament of marriage with several of that time signified the multitude that should be hereafter made subject unto God in all nations of the earth, so the Sacrament of marriage with one of our times signifies the unity of us all made subject to God, which shall be hereafter in one Heavenly City. Therefore as to serve two or more, so to pass over from a living husband into marriage with another, was neither lawful then, nor is it lawful now, nor will it ever be lawful. Forsooth to apostatize from the One God, and to go into adulterous superstition of another, is ever an evil. Therefore, not even for the sake of a more numerous family did our Saints do, what the Roman Cato is said to have done, to give up his wife, during his own life, to fill even another's house with sons. Forsooth in the marriage of one woman the sanctity of the Sacrament is of more avail than the fruitfulness of the womb.

22. If, therefore, even they who are united in marriage only for the purpose of begetting, for which purpose marriage was instituted, are not compared with the Fathers, seeking their very sons in a way far other than do these; forasmuch as Abraham, being bidden to slay his son, fearless and devoted, spared not his only son, whom from out of great despair he had received save that he laid down his hand, when He forbade him, at Whose command he had lifted it up; it remains that we consider, whether at least continent persons among us are to be compared to those Fathers who were married; unless haply now these are to be preferred to them, to whom we have not yet found persons to compare. For there was a greater good in their marriage, than is the proper good of marriage: to which without doubt the good of Continence is to be preferred: because they sought not sons from marriage by such duty as these are led by, from a certain

sense of mortal nature requiring succession against decease. And, whoso denies this to be good he knows not God, the Creator of all things good, from things heavenly even unto things earthly, from things immortal even unto things mortal. But neither are beasts altogether without this sense of begetting, and chiefly birds, whose care of building nests meets us at once, and a certain likeness to marriages, in order to beget and nurture together. But those men, with mind far holier, surpassed this affection of mortal nature, the chastity whereof in its own kind, there being added thereto the worship of God, as some have understood, is set forth as bearing first thirty-fold; who sought sons of their marriage for the sake of Christ; in order to distinguish His race after the flesh from all nations: even as God was pleased to order, that this above the rest should avail to prophesy of Him, in that it was foretold of what race also, and of what nation, He should hereafter come in the flesh. Therefore, it was a far greater good than the chaste marriages of believers among us, which father Abraham knew in his own thigh, under which he bade his servant to put his hand, that he might take an oath concerning the wife, whom his son was to marry. For putting his hand under the thigh of a man, and swearing by the God of Heaven, what else did he signify, than that in that Flesh, which derived its origin from that thigh, the God of Heaven would come? Therefore marriage is a good, wherein married persons are so much the better, in proportion as they fear God with greater chastity and faithfulness, especially if the sons, whom they desire after the flesh, they also bring up after the spirit.

23. Nor, in that the Law orders a man to be purified even after intercourse with a wife, doth it show it to be sin: unless it be that which is allowed by way of pardon, which also, being in excess, hinders prayers. But, as the Law sets many things in sacraments and shadows of things to come; a certain as it were material formless state of the seed, which having received form will hereafter produce the body of man, is set to signify a life formless, and untaught: from which formless state, forasmuch as it behooves that man be cleansed by form and teaching of learning; as a sign of this, that purification was ordered after the emission of seed. For neither in sleep also doth it take place through sin. And yet there also a purification was commanded. Or, if any think this also to be sin, thinking that it comes not to pass save from some lust of this kind, which without doubt is false; what? are the ordinary menses also of women sins? And yet from these the same old Law commanded that they should be cleansed by expiation; for no other cause, save the material formless state itself, in that which, when conception hath taken place, is added as it were to build up the body, and for this reason, when it flows without form, the Law would have signified by it a soul without form of discipline, flowing and loose in an unseemly manner. And that this ought to receive form, it signifies, when it commands such flow of the body to be purified. Lastly, what? to die, is that also a sin? or, to bury a dead person, is it not also a good work of humanity? and yet a purification was commanded even on occasion of this also; because also a dead body, life abandoning it, is not sin, but signifies the sin of a soul abandoned by righteousness.

24. Marriage, I say, is a good, and may be, by sound reason, defended against all calumnies. But with the marriage of the holy fathers, I inquire not what marriage, but what continence, is on a level: or rather not marriage with marriage; for it is an equal gift in all cases given to the mortal nature of men; but men who use marriage, forasmuch as I find not, to compare with other men who used marriage in a far other spirit, we must require what continent persons admit of being compared with those married persons. Unless, haply, Abraham could not contain from marriage, for the sake of the kingdom of heaven, he who, for the sake of the kingdom of heaven, could fearless sacrifice his only pledge of offspring, for whose sake marriage was dear!

25. Forsooth continence is a virtue, not of the body, but of the soul. But the virtues of the soul are sometimes shown in work, sometimes lie hid in habit, as the virtue of martyrdom shone forth and appeared by enduring sufferings; but how many are there of the same virtue of mind, unto whom trial is wanting, whereby what is within, in the sight of God, may go forth also into the sight of men, and not to men begin to exist, but only become known? For there was already in Job patience, which God knew, and to which He bore witness: but it became known unto men by test of trial: and what lay hid within was not produced, but shown, by the things that were brought on him from without. Timothy also certainly had the virtue of abstaining from wine, which Paul took not from him, by advising him to use a moderate portion of wine, "for the sake of his stomach

and his often infirmities," otherwise he taught him a deadly lesson, that for the sake of the health of the body there should be a loss of virtue in the soul: but because what he advised could take place with safety to that virtue, the profit of drinking was so left free to the body, as that the habit of continence continued in the soul. For it is the habit itself, whereby anything is done, when there is need; but when it is not done, it can be done, only there is no need. This habit, in the matter of that continence which is from sexual intercourse, they have not, unto whom it is said, "If they contain not, let them be married." But this they have, unto whom it is said, "Whoso can receive, let him receive." Thus have perfect souls used earthly goods, that are necessary for something else, through this habit of continence, so as, by it, not to be bound by them, and so as by it, to have power also not to use them, in case there were no need. Nor doth any use them well, save who hath power also not to use them. Many indeed with more ease practice abstinence, so as not to use, than practice temperance, so as to use well. But no one can wisely use them, save who can also continently not use them. From this habit Paul also said, "I know both to abound, and to suffer want." Forsooth to suffer want is the part of any men so ever; but to know to suffer want is the part of great men. So, also, to abound, who cannot? but to know also to abound, is not, save of those, whom abundance corrupts not.

26. But, in order that it may be more clearly understood, how there may be virtue in habit, although it be not in work, I speak of an example, about which no Catholic Christian can doubt. For that our Lord Jesus Christ in truth of flesh hungered and thirsted, ate and

drank, no one doubts of such as out of the Gospel are believers. What, then, was there not in Him the virtue of continence from meat and drink, as great as in John Baptist? "For John came neither eating nor drinking; and they said, He hath a devil; the Son of Man came both eating and drinking; and they said, "Lo, a glutton and wine-bibber, a friend of publicans and sinners." What, are not such things said also against them of His household, our fathers, from another kind of using of things earthy, so far as pertains to sexual intercourse; "Lo, men lustful and unclean, lovers of women and lewdness?" And yet as in Him that was not true, although it were true that He abstained not, even as John, from eating and drinking, for Himself saith most plainly and truly, "John came, not eating, nor drinking; the Son of Man came eating and drinking:" so neither is this true in these Fathers; although there hath come now the Apostle of Christ, not wedded, nor begetting, so that the heathen say of him, He was a magician; but there came then the Prophet of Christ, marrying and begetting sons, so that the Manichees say of him, He was a man fond of women: "And wisdom," saith He, "hath been justified of her children." What the Lord there added, after He had thus spoken of John and of Himself; "But wisdom," saith He, "hath been justified of her children." Who see that the virtue of continence ought to exist even in the habit of the soul, but to be shown forth in deed, according to opportunity of things and times; even as the virtue of patience of holy martyrs appeared in deed; but of the rest equally holy was in habit. Wherefore, even as there is not unequal desert of patience in Peter, who suffered, and in John, who suffered not; so there is not unequal desert of continence in John who made no trial of marriage, and in Abraham, who begat sons. For both the celibate of the one, and the marriage estate of the other, did service as soldiers to Christ, as times were allotted; but John had continence in work also, but Abraham in habit alone.

27. Therefore at that time, when the Law also, following upon the days of the Patriarchs, pronounced accursed, whoso raised not up seed in Israel, even he, who could, put it not forth, but yet possessed it. But from the period that the fullness of time hath come, that it should be said, "Whoso can receive, let him receive," from that period even unto this present, and from henceforth even unto the end, whoso hath, worketh: whoso shall be unwilling to work, let him not falsely say, that he hath. And through this means, they, who corrupt good manners by evil communications, with empty and vain craft, say to a Christian man exercising continence, and refusing marriage, What then, are you better than Abraham? But let him not, upon hearing this, be troubled; neither let him dare to say, "Better," nor let him fall away from his purpose: for the one he saith not truly, the other he doth not rightly. But let him say, I indeed am not better than Abraham, but the chastity of the unmarried is better than the chastity of marriage; whereof Abraham had one in use, both in habit. For he lived chastely in the marriage state: but it was in his power to be chaste without marriage, but at that time it behooved not. But I with more ease use not marriage, which Abraham used, than so use marriage as Abraham used it: and therefore I am better than those, who through incontinence of mind cannot do what I do; not than those, who, on account of difference of time, did not do what I do. For what I now do, they would have done better, if it had been to be done

at that time; but what they did, I should not so do, although it were now to be done. Or, if he feels and knows himself to be such, as that, (the virtue of continence being preserved and continued in the habit of his mind, in case he had descended unto the use of marriage from some duty of religion,) he should be such an husband, and such a father, as Abraham was; let him dare to make plain answer to that captious questioner, and to say, I am not indeed better than Abraham, only in this kind of continence, of which he was not void, although it appeared not: but I am such, not having other than he, but doing other. Let him say this plainly: forasmuch as, even if he shall wish to glory, he will not be a fool, for he saith the truth. But if he spare, lest any think of him above what he sees him, or hears anything of him; let him remove from his own person the knot of the question, and let him answer, not concerning the man, but concerning the thing itself, and let him say, Whoso hath so great power is such as Abraham. But it may happen that the virtue of continence is less in his mind, who uses not marriage, which Abraham used: but yet it is greater than in his mind, who on this account held chastity of marriage, in that he could not a greater. Thus also let the unmarried woman, whose thoughts are of the things of the Lord, that she may be holy both in body and spirit, when she shall have heard that shameless questioner saying, What, then, are you better than Sara? answer, I am better, but than those, who are void of the virtue of continence, which I believe not of Sara: she therefore together with this virtue did what was suited to that time, from which I am free, that in my body also may appear, what she kept in her mind.

28. Therefore, if we compare the things themselves, we may no way doubt that the chastity of continence is better than marriage chastity, whilst yet both are good: but when we compare the persons, he is better, who hath a greater good than another. Further, he who hath a greater of the same kind, hath also that which is less; but he, who only hath what is less, assuredly hath not that which is greater. For in sixty, thirty also are contained, not sixty also in thirty. But not to work from out that which he hath, stands in the allotment of duties, not in the want of virtues: forasmuch as neither is he without the good of mercy, who finds not wretched persons such as he may mercifully assist.

29. And there is this further, that men are not rightly compared with men in regard of someone good. For it may come to pass, that one hath not what another hath, but hath another thing, which must be esteemed of more value. The good of obedience is better than of continence. For marriage is in no place condemned by authority of our Scriptures, but disobedience is in no place acquitted. If therefore there be set before us a virgin about to continue so, but yet disobedient, and a married woman who could not continue a virgin, but yet obedient, which shall we call better? shall it be (the one) less praiseworthy, than if she were a virgin, or (the other) worthy of blame, even as she is a virgin? So, if you compare a drunken virgin with a sober married woman, who can doubt to pass the same sentence? Forsooth marriage and virginity are two goods, whereof the one is greater; but sobriety and drunkenness, even as obedience and stubbornness, are, the one good, and the other evil. But it is better to have all goods even in a less degree,

than great good with great evil: forasmuch as in the goods of the body also it is better to have the stature of Zacchæus with sound health, than that of Goliah with fever.

30. The right question plainly is, not whether a virgin every way disobedient is to be compared to an obedient married woman, but a less obedient to a more obedient: forasmuch as that also of marriage is chastity, and therefore a good, but less than virginal. Therefore if the one, by so much less in the good of obedience, as she is greater in the good of chastity, be compared with the other, which of them is to be preferred that person judges, who in the first place comparing chastity itself and obedience, sees that obedience is in a certain way the mother of all virtues. And therefore, for this reason, there may be obedience without virginity, because virginity is of counsel, not of precept. But I call that obedience, whereby precepts are complied with. And, therefore, there may be obedience to precepts without virginity, but not without chastity. For it pertains unto chastity, not to commit fornication, not to commit adultery, to be defiled by no unlawful intercourse: and whoso observe not these, do contrary to the precepts of God, and on this account are banished from the virtue of obedience. But there may be virginity without obedience, on this account, because it is possible for a woman, having received the counsel of virginity, and having guarded virginity, to slight precepts: even as we have known many sacred virgins, talkative, curious, drunken, litigious, covetous, proud: all which are contrary to precepts, and slay one, even as Eve herself, by the crime of disobedience. Wherefore not only is the obedient to be preferred to the disobedient, but a more

obedient married woman to a less obedient virgin.

31. From this obedience that Father, who was not without a wife, was prepared to be without an only son, and that slain by himself. For I shall not without due cause call him an only son, concerning whom he heard the Lord say, "In Isaac shall there be called for thee a seed." Therefore how much sooner would he hear it, that he should be even without a wife, if this he were bidden? Wherefore it is not without reason that we often consider, that some of both sexes, containing from all sexual intercourse, are negligent in obeying precepts, after having with so great warmth caught at the not making use of things that are allowed. Whence who doubts that we do not rightly compare unto the excellence of those holy fathers and mothers begetting sons, the men and women of our time, although free from all intercourse, yet in virtue of obedience inferior: even if there had been wanting to those men in habit of mind also, what is plain in the deed of the latter. Therefore let these follow the Lamb, boys singing the new song, as it is written in the Apocalypse, "who have not defiled themselves with women:" for no other reason than that they have continued virgins. Nor let them on this account think themselves better than the first holy fathers, who used marriage, so to speak, after the fashion of marriage. Forsooth the use of it is such, as that, if in it there hath taken place through carnal intercourse aught which exceeds necessity of begetting, although in a way that deserves pardon, there is pollution. For what doth pardon expiate, if that advance cause no pollution whatever? From which pollution it were strange if boys following the Lamb were free, unless they continued virgins.

32. Therefore the good of marriage throughout all nations and all men stands in the occasion of begetting, and faith of chastity: but, so far as pertains unto the People of God, also in the sanctity of the Sacrament, by reason of which it is unlawful for one who leaves her husband, even when she has been put away, to be married to another, so long as her husband lives, no not even for the sake of bearing children: and, whereas this is the alone cause, wherefore marriage takes place, not even where that very thing, wherefore it takes place, follows not, is the marriage bond loosed, save by the death of the husband or wife. In like manner as if there take place an ordination of clergy in order to form a congregation of people, although the congregation of people follow not, yet there remains in the ordained persons the Sacrament of Ordination; and if, for any fault, any be removed from his office, he will not be without the Sacrament of the Lord once for all set upon him, albeit continuing unto condemnation. Therefore, that marriage takes place for the sake of begetting children, the Apostle is a witness thus, "I will," says he, "that the younger women be married." And, as though it were said to him, For what purpose? straightway he added, "to have children, to be mothers of families." But unto the faith of chastity pertains that saying, "The wife hath not power of her own body, but the husband: likewise also the husband hath not power of his own body, but the wife." But unto the sanctity of the Sacrament that saying, "The wife not to depart from her husband, but, in case she shall have departed, to remain unmarried, or to be reconciled to her husband: and let not the husband put away his wife." All

these are goods, on account of which marriage is a good; offspring, faith, sacrament. But now, at this time, not to seek offspring after the flesh, and by this means to maintain a certain perpetual freedom from every such work, and to be made subject after a spiritual manner unto one Husband Christ, is assuredly better and holier; provided, that is, men so use that freedom, as it is written, so as to have their thoughts of the things of the Lord, how to please the Lord; that is, that Continence at all times do take thought, that obedience fall not short in any matter: and this virtue, as the root-virtue, and (as it is wont to be called) the womb, and clearly universal, the holy fathers of old exercised in deed; but that Continence they possessed in habit of mind. Who assuredly, through that obedience, whereby they were just and holy, and ever prepared unto every good work, even if they were bidden to abstain from all sexual intercourse, would perform it. For how much more easily could they, at the bidding or exhortation of God, not use sexual intercourse, who, as an act of obedience, could slay the child, for the begetting of which alone they used the ministry of sexual intercourse?

33. And, the case being thus, enough and more than enough answer has been made to the heretics, whether they be Manichees, or whosoever other that bring false charges against the Fathers of the Old Testament, on the subject of their having several wives, thinking this a proof whereby to convict them of incontinence: provided, that is, that they perceive, that that is no sin, which is committed neither against nature, in that they used those women not for wantonness, but for the begetting of children: nor against custom, forasmuch as such things were usually done at those times: nor against command,

forasmuch as they were forbidden by no law. But such as used women unlawfully, either the divine sentence in those Scriptures convicts them, or the reading sets them forth for us to condemn and shun, not to approve or imitate.

34. But those of ours who have wives we advise, with all our power, that they dare not to judge of those holy fathers after their own weakness, comparing, as the Apostle says, themselves with themselves; and therefore, not understanding how great strength the soul hath, doing service unto righteousness against lusts, that it acquiesce not in carnal motions of this sort, or suffer them to glide on or advance unto sexual intercourse beyond the necessity of begetting children, so far as the order of nature, so far as the use of custom, so far as the decrees of laws prescribe. Forsooth it is on this account that men have this suspicion concerning those fathers, in that they themselves have either chosen marriage through incontinence, or use their wives with intemperance. But however let such as are continent, either men, who, on the death of their wives, or, women, who, on the death of their husbands, or both, who, with mutual consent, have vowed continence unto God, know that to them indeed there is due a greater recompense than marriage chastity demands; but, (as regards) the marriages of the holy Fathers, who were joined after the manner of prophecy, who neither in sexual intercourse sought aught save children, nor in children themselves aught save what should set forward Christ coming hereafter in the flesh, not only let them not despise them in comparison of their own purpose, but let them without any doubting prefer them even to their own purpose.

35. Boys also and virgins dedicating unto God actual chastity we do before all things admonish, that they be aware that they must guard their life meanwhile upon earth with so great humility, by how much the more what they have vowed is heavenly. Forsooth it is written, "How great so ever thou art, by so much humble thyself in all things." Therefore it is our part to say something of their greatness, it is their part to have thought of great humility. Therefore, except certain, those holy fathers and mothers who were married, than whom these although they be not married are not better, for this reason, that, if they were married, they would not be equal, let them not doubt that they surpass all the rest of this time, either married, or after trial made of marriage, exercising continence; not so far as Anna surpasses Susanna; but so far as Mary surpasses both. I am speaking of what pertains unto the holy chastity itself of the flesh; for who knows not, what other deserts Mary hath? Therefore let them add to this so high purpose conduct suitable, that they may have an assured security of the surpassing reward; knowing of a truth, that, unto themselves and unto all the faithful, beloved and chosen members of Christ, coming many from the East, and from the West, although shining with light of glory that differed one from another, according to their deserts, there is this great gift bestowed in common, to sit down in the kingdom of God with Abraham, and Isaac, and Jacob, who not for the sake of this world, but for the sake of Christ, were husbands, for the sake of Christ were fathers.

www.ingramcontent.com/pod-product-compliance
Lightning Source LLC
Chambersburg PA
CBHW052043070526
44584CB00018B/2590